JUSTINIAN I THE PEASANT BOY WHO BECAME EMPEROR

BIOGRAPHY FOR KIDS
CHILDREN'S BIOGRAPHY BOOKS

BABY PROFESSOR
EDUCATION KIDS

Speedy Publishing LLC

40 E. Main St. #1156

Newark, DE 19711

www.speedypublishing.com

Copyright 2017

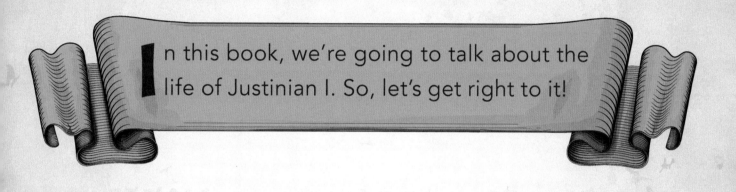

In this book, we're going to talk about the life of Justinian I. So, let's get right to it!

JUSTINIAN I

WHO WAS JUSTINIAN I?

Justinian I was originally named Flavius Peterus Sabbatius and was born in 482 AD and died in 565 AD. He changed his name to Justinian after his uncle's name of Justin. Just as his uncle had done, Justinian rose from a very humble background to become a great leader.

He was an emperor during the late period of the Roman and Byzantium Empire. He made significant contributions in art and also architecture. He was a champion of legal reform as well.

THE FAMOUS 1500 YEAR OLD PORTRAIT OF THE EMPEROR JUSTINIAN AND BISHOP MAXIMIAN

Although he was not a soldier himself, he commanded a fighting force that captured a large amount of land for the empire. Justinian believed in Christianity and he showed his faith in all of his endeavors. Up until his time, emperors had been military leaders and politicians but they weren't revered as spiritual leaders.

Thanks to the historian Procopius who wrote about Justinian's life, we know a great deal about his time as emperor, which lasted 38 years. His reign from 527 AD through 565 AD was considered to be a Golden Age for the Byzantium Empire.

ANCIENT BYZANTIUM MOSAIC
FRESCO IN KARIYE MOSQUE

THE RUINS OF TAURESIUM

JUSTINIAN'S EARLY LIFE

Justinian was born in 482 AD in the city of Tauresium, which was in Macedonia. He didn't have a royal background. His mother and father were peasants. His mother's name was Vigilantia and her brother's name was Justin. It was through his uncle Justin that Justinian rose to the throne in a very unusual way.

His uncle was part of the Excubitor, which was the guard that protected the emperor. As the emperor's bodyguard, Justin developed a close friendship with the emperor Anastasius who had no heirs of his own. An ambitious man, Justin was befriended by other strong leaders as well as the emperor. When the emperor passed away in 518 AD, Justin grabbed the power and became emperor.

JUSTIN I, PORTRAIT ON A COIN

CONSULAR DIPTYCH OF JUSTIN

Justin favored his nephew. He adopted the young boy and took him to the capital city of Constantinople. There, Justinian received a quality education. He became literate and in addition to mastering reading and writing, he learned about the law and Roman history. While his uncle Justin was emperor, Justinian became one of his close advisors and in 521 AD at the age of 39, he was awarded the position of Consul, which gave him a lot of executive power. Soon he became the commander of the army in the eastern part of the empire.

JUSTINIAN AND THEODORA

Due to his uncle, Justinian had risen in society. Then, he fell in love with an actress whose name was Theodora. At that time, actresses were considered to be very low-level members of society and they were not allowed to marry into high society. However, Justinian loved Theodora and had the laws changed.

MOSAIC OF THEODORA

He married her in 525 AD when he was 43 and she was 28. Theodora was very intelligent and Justinian trusted her advice on all matters.

JUSTINIAN

JUSTINIAN BECOMES EMPEROR

When his beloved uncle passed away in 527 AD, Justinian became emperor with Theodora as his co-regent, which means she helped him to rule. Justinian was unhappy with the condition of the empire. The empire needed to be completely remade. It needed legal and military changes and it also needed its buildings rebuilt, since many had cracks and peeling paint.

He wanted the Byzantium Empire to be great once more and he set out to do it. He was a Christian and believed that the church should work hand in hand with the state in order to bring harmony to the empire.

SANGARIUS BRIDGE BUILT BY JUSTINIAN I

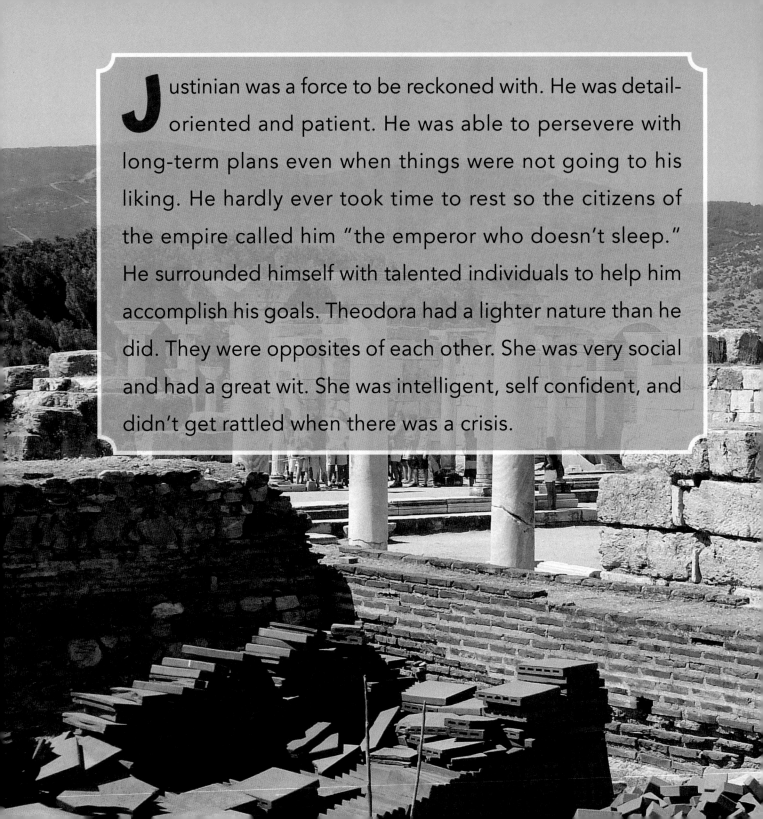

Justinian was a force to be reckoned with. He was detail-oriented and patient. He was able to persevere with long-term plans even when things were not going to his liking. He hardly ever took time to rest so the citizens of the empire called him "the emperor who doesn't sleep." He surrounded himself with talented individuals to help him accomplish his goals. Theodora had a lighter nature than he did. They were opposites of each other. She was very social and had a great wit. She was intelligent, self confident, and didn't get rattled when there was a crisis.

RUINS OF BASILICA OF
BYZANTINE EMPEROR JUSTINIAN

WAR SCENE FRESCO (BYZANTINE EMPIRE)

EXPANDING THE EMPIRE

At one time, the Western Roman Empire and the Eastern Roman Empire, also called the Byzantium Empire, had been one unified empire. Justinian sent out two generals to command his massive armies. His goal was to reunite these two empires and he almost succeeded.

Through the work of his general Belisarius and his other general Narses, the empire was able to get back almost all of the regions that had been lost during the collapse of the western section of the previous Roman Empire.

GENERAL BELISARIUS

THE EASTERN ROMAN EMPIRE (RED)
DURING THE REIGN OF JUSTINIAN I

During this time, the Vandals had control of Africa and Justinian dispatched his generals and soldiers to take the region back in 533 AD. He negotiated a peace treaty with his rivals the Persians in the eastern regions. His generals and soldiers conquered Slavic and Arabic kingdoms in quick succession.

The most difficult and longest battle to regain ground was with the Goths who had taken over the lands of Italy. The battle began in 535 AD and lasted for over 25 years. Eventually, the Goths were defeated and Italy and Rome were once again part of the empire. However, the cost had been great.

GOTHIC WAR

These military campaigns took a huge amount of money and the empire's treasury didn't have much left in it. The people had been taxed to a great degree and they were upset.

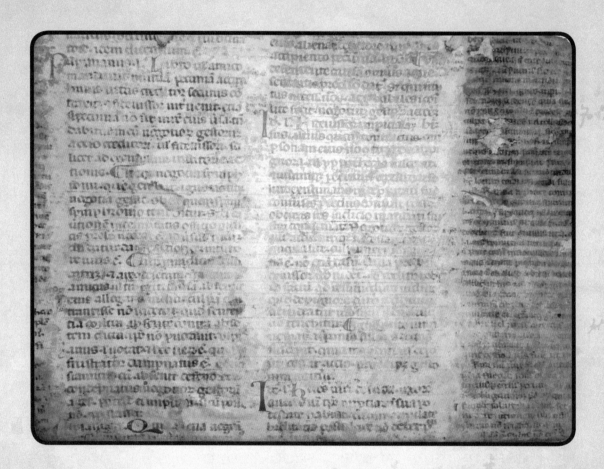

GLOSSED COPY OF JUSTINIAN'S DIGESTA

THE JUSTINIAN CODE

While battles were going on throughout the empire, Justinian also began work on codifying Roman law. He founded three schools of law and also established a commission. Their task was to take all the Roman laws and reorganize them into a clear, authoritative structure of laws for the entire empire.

The new code of laws was called the Justinian Code. This new code favored Christians because it was Justinian's belief that Christianity was the "right way to worship God."

ATHENS

He wasn't tolerant of heretics or those who didn't profess a belief in God. He swiftly closed down the University in the city of Athens, because it was a hub for pagan practices.

However, on the other hand, he made it easier to set Christian slaves free and he made sure that Christian women and their children had legal recourse.

MEGALITHS - SOME ARE BELIEVED TO HAVE RELIGIOUS SIGNIFICANCE BY THE PAGANS

RELIGION, THE ARTS, AND ARCHITECTURE

In addition to his legal and military achievements, Justinian united religion, the arts, and architecture as he sought to rebuild the structures that had made the former Roman Empire so glorious. He constructed majestic structures all around the empire including 25 basilicas just in the capital city of Constantinople.

THE BASILICA CISTERN

The Sancta Sophia, which means "Holy Wisdom," was the jewel of all the architecture during that period.

HAGIA SOPHIA

THE CEILING OF HAGIA SOPHIA

It is known today as the Hagia Sophia and was converted to a mosque many centuries after it was built as the first Christian cathedral of the Byzantium Empire.

RIOTS DURING THE CHARIOT RACES

Even though Justinian had achieved a great deal throughout his reign, the citizens weren't pleased with him. One of the reasons was that he had taxed the people heavily in order to fund his military campaigns as well as his building renovation projects.

THE HIPPODROME

During a competitive chariot race in the year 532 AD, a riot broke out. There were two rival teams competing against each other in the race.

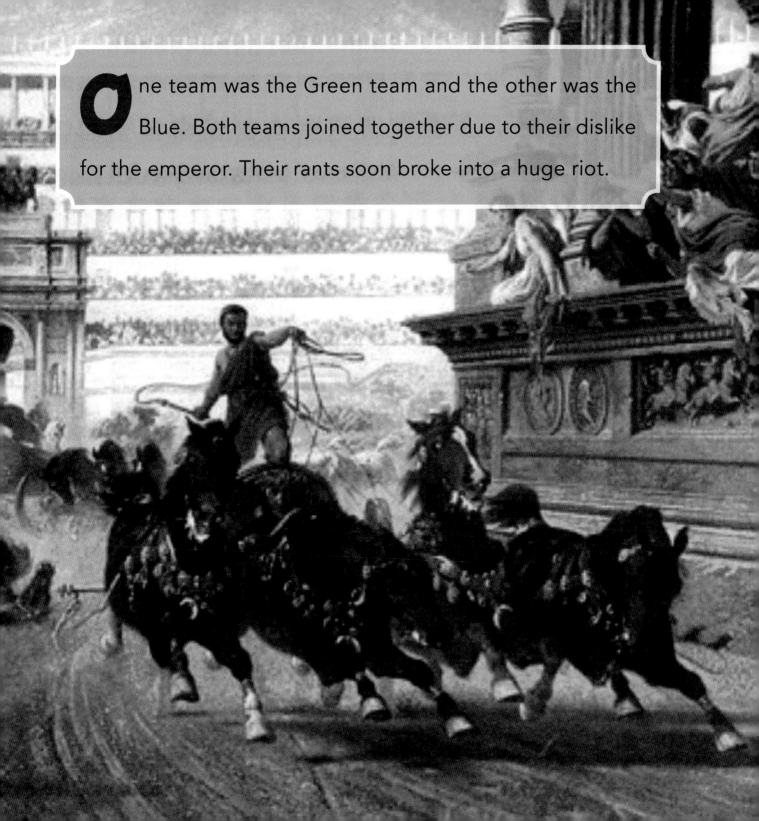

One team was the Green team and the other was the Blue. Both teams joined together due to their dislike for the emperor. Their rants soon broke into a huge riot.

ANCIENT CONSTANTINOPLE

They began to attack Justinian's palace grounds and burn down buildings in the capital city of Constantinople. Justinian's nerves were tested and he wanted to escape, but because of the advice of his clear-thinking wife Theodora, he decided to send in soldiers and fight back. However, in order to end the unrest about 30,000 rioters met their deaths.

JUSTINIAN'S DEATH

Justinian passed away in 565 AD at the age of 83 years old, which was a very old age for that time period. He had ruled for 38 years, but he and Theodora had no heir so his nephew took the position of emperor.

THE HEALING OF JUSTINIAN

SOLIDUS OF JUSTIN II

His nephew was named Justin II. Unfortunately, the lands that Justinian had regained began to crumble within two years. They were conquered but never really joined with the other lands belonging to the empire.

JUSTINIAN THE GREAT'S LEGACY

Justinian I came from humble beginnings to become one of the greatest emperors the world had ever known. During his reign, he regained most of the lands that had been lost during the collapse of the Roman Empire and expanded the territories of the Byzantium Empire.

A devout Christian, he had Roman Law reorganized into a new code that was later called the Justinian Code. He was also the driving force behind the construction of many beautiful buildings, including the building that is known today as the Hagia Sophia.

Awesome! Now that you've read about the life of Justinian I, you may want to read more about the ancient history of Rome before the Christian era in the Baby Professor book Bloody Entertainment in the Roman Arenas – Ancient History Picture Books.

BLUE MOSQUE AND HAGIA SOFIA